BASIC/NOT BORING

LANGUAGE, WRITING, & USAGE

Grades 2-3

Inventive Exercises to Sharpen
Skills and Raise Achievement

Series Concept & Development
by Imogene Forte & Marjorie Frank
Exercises by Laurie Grupé

Incentive Publications, Inc.
Nashville, Tennessee

About the cover:
Bound resist, or tie dye, is the most ancient known method of fabric surface design. The brilliance of the basic tie dye design on this cover reflects the possibilities that emerge from the mastery of basic skills.

Illustrated by Kathleen Bullock
Cover art by Mary Patricia Deprez, dba Tye Dye Mary®
Cover design by Marta Drayton, Joe Shibley, and W. Paul Nance
Edited by Anna Quinn

ISBN 0-86530-393-2

Copyright ©1998 by Incentive Publications, Inc., Nashville, TN. All rights reserved. No part of this publication may be reproduced, stored in a retrieval system, or transmitted in any form or by any means (electronic, mechanical, photocopying, recording, or otherwise) without written permission from Incentive Publications, Inc., with the exception below.

Pages labeled with the statement **©1998 by Incentive Publications, Inc., Nashville, TN** are intended for reproduction. Permission is hereby granted to the purchaser of one copy of **BASIC/NOT BORING LANGUAGE, WRITING, & USAGE Grades 2–3** to reproduce these pages in sufficient quantities for meeting the purchaser's own classroom needs only.

PRINTED IN THE UNITED STATES OF AMERICA

TABLE OF CONTENTS

Introduction: Celebrate Basic Language Skills 7
Skills Checklist 8

Skills Exercises 9
The Carnival Comes to Town . . . (Nouns & Verbs) 10
Milton the Magnificent! . . . (Nouns) 12
A Great Balancing Act . . . (Proper Nouns) 13
Step Right Up! . . . (Plural Nouns) 14
Getting Ready for the Show . . . (Possessive Nouns) 15
Monkey Action . . . (Verbs) 16
Take a Spin! . . . (Verb Tenses) 18
The Big Game . . . (Adjectives) 19
Clowning Around . . . (Comparative Adjectives) 20
Adventures on the High Wire . . . (Adverbs) 21
Leaping through Fire . . . (Complete Sentences) 22
Ring around Run-ons . . . (Run-on Sentences) 23
Ribbons around Run-ons . . . (Run-on Sentences) 24
Inside the Lion's Mouth . . . (Statements) 25
Unusual Talents . . . (Questions) 26
Watch out for Pirates! . . . (Exclamations) 27
A Bunch of Balloons . . . (Statements, Questions, & Exclamations) 28
Seven Silly Seals . . . (Sentence Parts) 29
In the Center Ring . . . (Sentence Parts) 30
Juggling for Contractions . . . (Contractions) 31
Ups & Downs . . . (Capitalization) 32

Aim for the Ducks . . . (Punctuation) 33

Quotes from the Circus Train . . . (Quotations) 34

Madame Mystery's Message . . . (Punctuation) 35

Mistakes on the Merry-Go-Round . . . (Capitalization & Punctuation) 36

A Letter to Ulysses . . . (Capitalization & Punctuation) 37

Weird, Wacky Mirrors . . . (Spelling) 38

Dancing with a Bear . . . (Spelling) 39

Sniffing out Mistakes . . . (Spelling) 40

Wonderful Carnival Words . . . (Writing: Descriptive Words) 41

Tempt Your Taste Buds . . . (Writing: Word Choice) 42

Come One, Come All! . . . (Writing: Poster) 43

Titles to Talk About . . . (Writing: Titles) 44

A Three-Ring Circus . . . (Writing: Generating & Organizing Ideas) 46

A Chat with the Fire-Eater . . . (Writing: Interview Questions) 48

Help for Handy . . . (Writing: Directions) 49

A Lion on the Loose! . . . (Writing: Directions) 50

Tina the Terrific . . . (Writing: Finishing a Story) 51

Fantastic Dreams . . . (Writing: Imaginative Piece) 52

A Letter from a Lion . . . (Writing: Letter) 53

Too Much of a Good Thing . . . (Writing: Eliminating Irrelevant Ideas) 54

Clowns up Close . . . (Writing: Character Descriptions) 56

Appendix

Language, Writing, & Usage Skills Test 58

Answer Key 62

CELEBRATE BASIC LANGUAGE SKILLS

Basic does not mean boring! There is certainly nothing dull about clever circus clowns, adventuresome animals, and daring circus acts. It is so much fun to . . .
   . . . watch mischievous monkeys, dancing bears, and balancing elephants
   . . . hold your breath for the high-wire act or the courageous fire-eater
   . . . enjoy clowns doing funny tricks
   . . . lead the lion trainer to a lion on the loose
   . . . imagine rides on pirate ships, circus trains, and wild roller coasters
   . . . think about what a lion would write in a letter
   . . . help a clown figure out how to put on her costume
   . . . watch jugglers balance toasters, telephones, teapots, and birthday cakes

These are just some of the adventures students can explore as they celebrate basic language skills. The idea of celebrating the basics is just what it sounds like—enjoying and improving language usage and writing skills. Each page invites young learners to try a high-interest, visually appealing exercise that will sharpen one specific word skill. This is not just an ordinary fill-in-the-blanks way to learn. These exercises are fun and surprising. Students will do the useful work of practicing language skills while they enjoy the excitement of circus adventures and characters.

The pages in this book can be used in many ways:
- to review or practice a skill with one student
- to sharpen the skill with a small or large group
- to start off a lesson on a particular skill
- to assess how well a student has mastered a skill

Each page has directions that are written simply. It is intended that an adult be available to help students read the information on the page, if needed. In most cases, the pages will be used best as a follow-up to a skill that has already been taught. The pages are excellent tools for immediate reinforcement of a concept.

As your students take on the challenges of these adventures with language usage and writing, they will grow! And as you watch them check off the basic language skills they've strengthened, you can celebrate with them.

The Skills Test

Use the skills test beginning on page 58 as a pretest and/or a post-test. This will help you check the students' mastery of basic language usage skills and will prepare them for success on achievement tests.

SKILLS CHECKLIST
LANGUAGE, WRITING, & USAGE, GRADES 2-3

✔	SKILL	PAGE(S)
	Identify and write nouns	10–15
	Identify and write verbs	10, 11, 16–18
	Identify, write, and capitalize proper nouns	13, 32, 36, 37
	Identify and write plural nouns	14
	Identify and write possessive nouns	15
	Identify and write adjectives (describing words)	19, 20
	Add er and est to adjectives to make comparisons	20
	Identify and use adverbs	21
	Identify complete sentences and fix sentence fragments	22
	Recognize and correct run-on sentences	23, 24
	Identify, capitalize, and punctuate statements	25, 28, 33, 35–37
	Identify, capitalize, and punctuate questions	26, 28, 33, 35–37
	Identify, capitalize, and punctuate exclamations	27, 28, 33, 36, 37
	Distinguish among statements, questions, and exclamations	28, 33, 34, 36, 37
	Identify subjects and predicates	29, 30
	Identify common contractions and the words that form them	31
	Capitalize words in sentences	32, 36, 37
	Identify different punctuation marks and their uses	33–35
	Identify and correct punctuation errors	35–37
	Find correctly spelled words; correct spelling errors	38–40
	Generate and organize ideas for writing	41–57
	Express original ideas clearly in writing	41–57
	Choose effective, interesting words for writing	41, 42
	Write phrases for a poster	43
	Create good titles for written selections	44, 45
	Use collected ideas to create a written piece	46, 47
	Create good questions	48
	Write ideas in sequence	49
	Write clear directions	49, 50
	Write a short imaginative piece	51, 52
	Write a short letter and envelope	53
	Eliminate excess ideas in a written piece	54, 55
	Write character descriptions	56, 57

LANGUAGE, WRITING, & USAGE

Grades 2-3

Skills Exercises

The Carnival Comes to Town

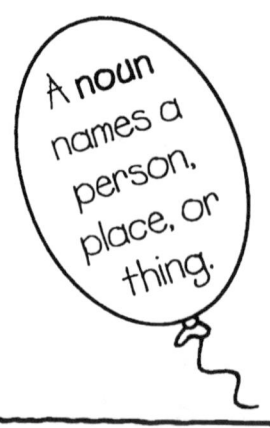

*A **noun** names a person, place, or thing.*

See the daring circus acts! Hop on the thrilling rides! Watch hilarious clowns!

Take a chance on winning great prizes! The carnival has come to town!

Look at the carnival on these two pages (pages 10 and 11). Choose the things that you would like to see and do. Write a list of your top 10 choices!

Top 10 Things to See

Write 10 nouns naming things you want to see.

1. _____
2. _____
3. _____
4. _____
5. _____
6. _____
7. _____
8. _____
9. _____
10. _____

Name _____

Use with page 11.

Nouns & Verbs

Copyright ©1998 by INCENTIVE PUBLICATIONS, Inc., Nashville, TN.
Basic Skills/Language, Writing, & Usage 2-3

The Carnival Comes to Town, cont.

*A **verb** shows action. It tells what someone is doing.*

Top 10 Things to Do
Write 10 verbs telling actions you want to do.

1. _____
2. _____
3. _____
4. _____
5. _____
6. _____
7. _____
8. _____
9. _____
10. _____

Name _____

Use with page 10.

Nouns & Verbs

Milton the Magnificent!

*A **noun** names a person, place, or thing.*

Milton wants to pull a surprise out of his hat. What will it be? Find the noun in each sentence and put a red line under it. Write the first letter of the noun in the matching blank below. Then draw the surprise in Milton's hand!

Abracadabra!

1. She is a good friend.
2. She never needs an umbrella.
3. She is not a zebra.
4. She has never lived in a zoo!
5. She's afraid of yaks.
6. She often sleeps in the kitchen.
7. She is not an iguana.
8. She has a sticky, pink tongue.
9. Her teeth are tiny and sharp.
10. She hates eating eggs.
11. Her curious nose sniffs everything!

__ __ __ __ __ __ __ __ __ __ __
1 2 3 4 5 6 7 8 9 10 11

Name _____

Nouns

A Great Balancing Act

The seals do a fantastic balancing act.

They can bounce and balance many balls at one time.

Look at the nouns on the balls. Which ones are proper nouns?

Give every proper noun a capital letter, and then color its ball.

A **proper noun** names a particular person, place, or thing. It begins with a capital letter.

Balls:
- mrs. clown
- bellview school
- seals
- dallas, texas
- carnival
- valentine's day
- leo lion
- july
- october
- monday
- zebra
- brooklyn bridge
- rizzo the clown
- main street
- milton
- trapeze
- magician
- friday
- colorado river
- thanksgiving

Name _____

Copyright ©1998 by Incentive Publications, Inc., Nashville, TN.
Basic Skills/Language, Writing, & Usage 2-3

Proper Nouns 13

Step Right Up!

A plural noun names more than one of something.

"Step right up!" "Win great prizes!" "It's so easy!"

Listen to the shouts along the carnival arcade. Look at all the prizes to win.

Clyde Clown would like to win more than one!

Write the plural form of each noun in the box under the picture.

mouse	bunny	bear	knife
camera	butterfly	puppy	turtle
fish	glass	radio	monkey
duck	pennant	hippo	

Name _____

14
Plural Nouns

Copyright ©1998 by Incentive Publications, Inc., Nashville, TN.
Basic Skills/Language, Writing, & Usage 2-3

Getting Ready for the Show

These cute little clowns are all dressed up for tonight's show.
It took a long time to get them ready.
Let's see what they are wearing!

Finish the sentences below.

Add **'s** in each space to show that the clown owns something.

Add 's to most nouns to show ownership.

Bubbles   Bebe   Babboo   Bobby

1. Bubbles is holding Bobby _____ bear.
2. Can you count Bebe _____ buttons and Babboo _____ bows?
3. Whose name is on Bobby _____ bib?
4. Bubbles likes his bottle better than Bebe _____ bonnet.
5. Look! Isn't Bobby _____ balloon big?
6. Babboo _____ booties are big enough for Bubbles.
7. There are spots on every clown _____ cheeks.
8. Everyone admires Bobby _____ hairdo.

Color the clowns and their costumes!

Name _____

Possessive Nouns

15

Copyright ©1998 by INCENTIVE PUBLICATIONS, Inc., Nashville, TN.
Basic Skills/Language, Writing, & Usage 2-3

Monkey Action

A verb shows action. It tells what someone is doing.

What is more fun than a barrel of monkeys? Not much!

This barrel holds a puzzle about the actions of monkeys.

Every word in the puzzle is a verb.

Use the clues and the words in the **Word Box** (on page 17) to find the right answers for the puzzle.

Filled-in letters in the crossword:
- 2 Down: SCRATCH
- 8 Across: CHATTER

Name _____

Use with page 17.

16 Verbs

Copyright ©1998 by Incentive Publications, Inc., Nashville, TN.
Basic Skills/Language, Writing, & Usage 2-3

Use these clues to finish the puzzle on page 16.
Every answer is a verb.

Down

1. Mongo always _____ and laughed at the other monkeys.
2. Have you noticed how much monkeys __scratch__ under their arms?
3. Morey Monkey always _____ the toes of the other monkeys.
9. Oops! He slipped out of the barrel and _____ to the ground.
10. Sometimes the monkeys _____ around in their food!
13. Did you see that monkey _____ a banana across the cage?

Across

4. How high can that monkey _____ ?
5. Watch her do a _____ off the bar!
6. When the monkey got a can of soda pop, all he did was _____ it.
7. Did the zoo keeper _____ Morey when the lunch was passed out?
8. Monkeys are noisy. They screech and __chatter__ .
11. Minnie _____ when the monkeys tease her.
12. Oh, no! That's too high! Don't _____ !
14. That flip turned into a _____ .
15. Monkeys _____ up bananas very fast.

WORD BOX
toss
shake
chatter
scratch
roll
gobble
tickles
reach
sobs
skip
tumbled
flip
flop
jump
teased

Name _____

Use with page 16.

Take a Spin!

Rule 1
Add ed to most verbs to show past tense. If a verb ends in e, drop the e and add ed.

Rule 2
If a one-syllable word ends in a consonant with a vowel before it, double the consonant and add ed.

The Clown-around Kids were having great fun on the spinning teacups. Oops! When they finished, they were very dizzy.

Read the rules about forming the past tense of verbs (like *finished*). Write each verb in the past tense.

If you followed Rule 1, color the cup or saucer yellow.
If you followed Rule 2, color the cup or saucer green.

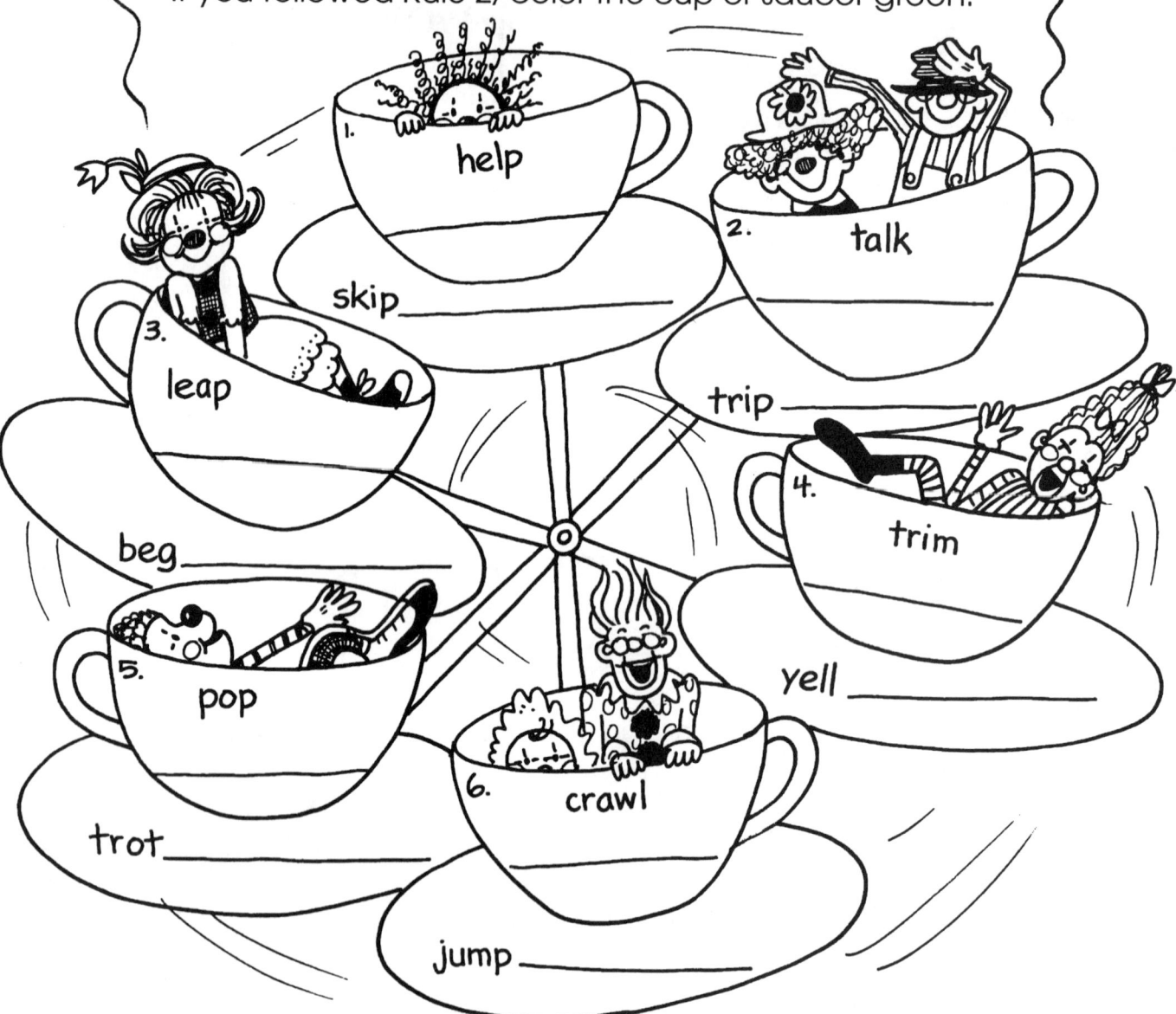

1. help
2. talk
3. leap
4. trim
5. pop
6. crawl

skip _____
trip _____
beg _____
yell _____
trot _____
jump _____

Name _____

18 Verb Tenses

Copyright ©1998 by Incentive Publications, Inc., Nashville, TN.
Basic Skills/Language, Writing, & Usage 2-3

The Big Game

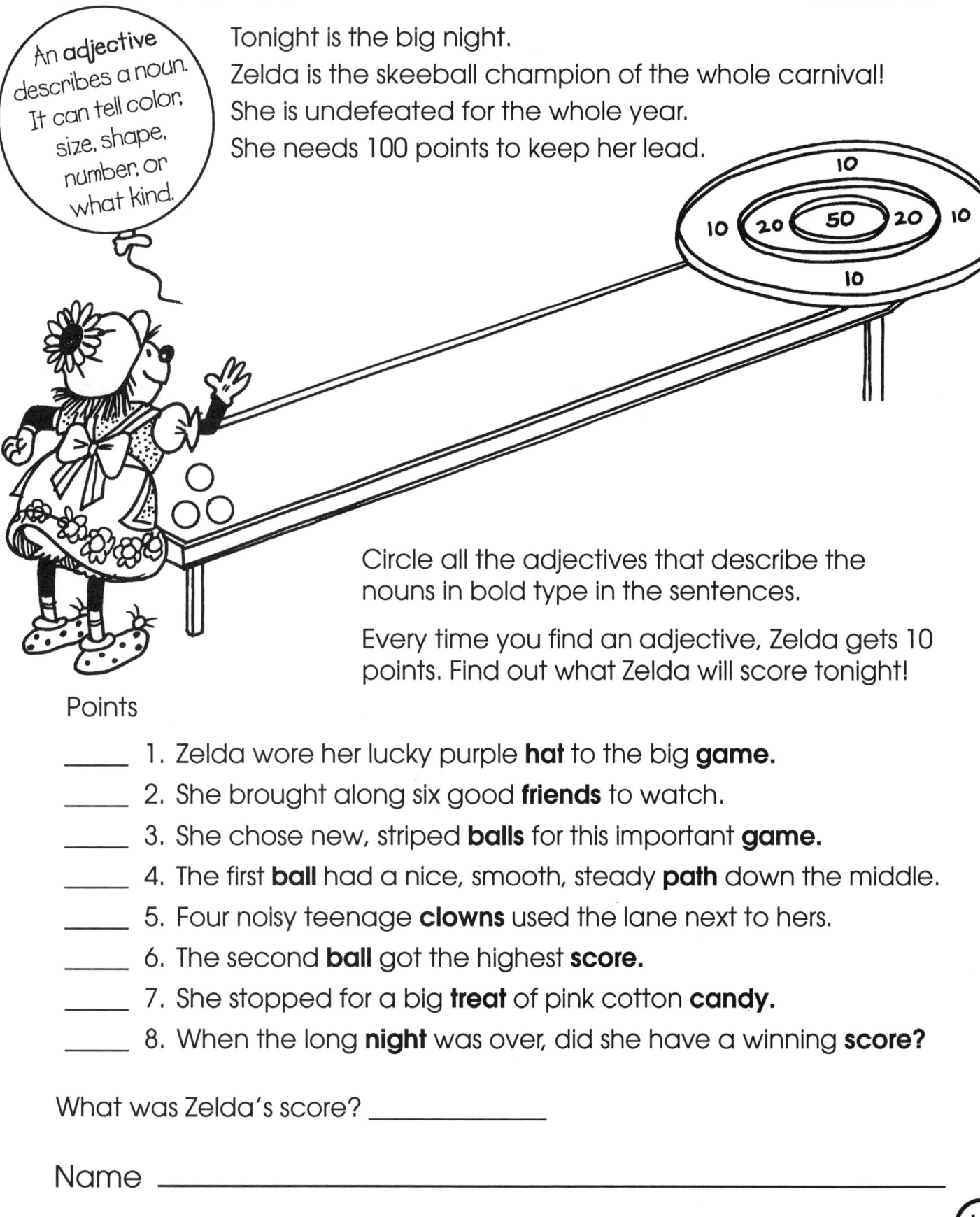

An adjective describes a noun. It can tell color, size, shape, number, or what kind.

Tonight is the big night.
Zelda is the skeeball champion of the whole carnival!
She is undefeated for the whole year.
She needs 100 points to keep her lead.

Circle all the adjectives that describe the nouns in bold type in the sentences.

Every time you find an adjective, Zelda gets 10 points. Find out what Zelda will score tonight!

Points

_____ 1. Zelda wore her lucky purple **hat** to the big **game.**

_____ 2. She brought along six good **friends** to watch.

_____ 3. She chose new, striped **balls** for this important **game.**

_____ 4. The first **ball** had a nice, smooth, steady **path** down the middle.

_____ 5. Four noisy teenage **clowns** used the lane next to hers.

_____ 6. The second **ball** got the highest **score.**

_____ 7. She stopped for a big **treat** of pink cotton **candy.**

_____ 8. When the long **night** was over, did she have a winning **score?**

What was Zelda's score? _____

Name _____

Clowning Around

Add **er** to an adjective to compare two objects. Add **est** to compare more than two objects.

Polly   Molly   Lolly

"My hat is biggest," Molly brags.
"My shoes are bigger," hollers Polly.
"Well, my hair is longer!" says Lolly.

The Clown-around Sisters are comparing some things.

Write the correct form of each word to make their comparisons correct.

1. Polly's shoes are _____ than Molly's. (large)
2. Whose nose is the _____ of all? (big)
3. Polly is _____ than Molly (tall) but _____ than Lolly. (short)
4. Whose feet are _____ ? (large)
5. Whose hair is _____ than Polly's? (long)
6. Molly's hair is _____ than Lolly's. (short)
7. Which hat has the _____ brim? (wide)
8. "I'm glad my hat is the _____ ," says Polly. (little)
9. "My cheeks are not any _____ than yours!" says Molly. (red)
10. Who thinks that Polly has the _____ shoes? (silly)

Name _____

Comparative Adjectives

Adventures on the High Wire

Amazing! Henrietta can walk on a skinny wire high off the ground!

It is a long, long way down if she falls.

Will she stay on the wire? Find out!

*An **adverb** describes a verb. It tells how, when, where, or how often something happened.*

As you read, circle the adverb in each sentence that tells the how, when, or where about the verb. The clue at the end of each sentence will help you.

1. Henrietta climbed slowly up the ladder to the wire. (Climbed how?)
2. She knew that she would start her act soon. (Would start when?)
3. She did not look down at the crowd. (Did not look where?)
4. Carefully, she stepped onto the wire. (Stepped how?)
5. She looked only ahead. (Looked where?)
6. She held on tightly to her umbrella. (Held how?)
7. She never felt nervous at the beginning. (Felt how often?)
8. She frequently felt nervous halfway across. (Felt how often?)
9. She began to breathe deeply to relax. (Breathed how?)
10. Soon she would reach the other side. (Would reach when?)
11. Suddenly she sneezed. (Sneezed how?)
12. She fell rapidly toward the ground. (Fell how?)
13. It was good that she landed safely in the net. (Landed how?)
14. "Tomorrow I will stay on the wire!" she said. (Will stay when?)

Name _____

Leaping through Fire

A complete sentence has a naming part and an action part.

It's so much fun to watch this act!
Waldo has trained his dogs to leap through burning hoops.
The dogs don't even act afraid (except for one).
Finish each sentence fragment to make it a complete sentence.

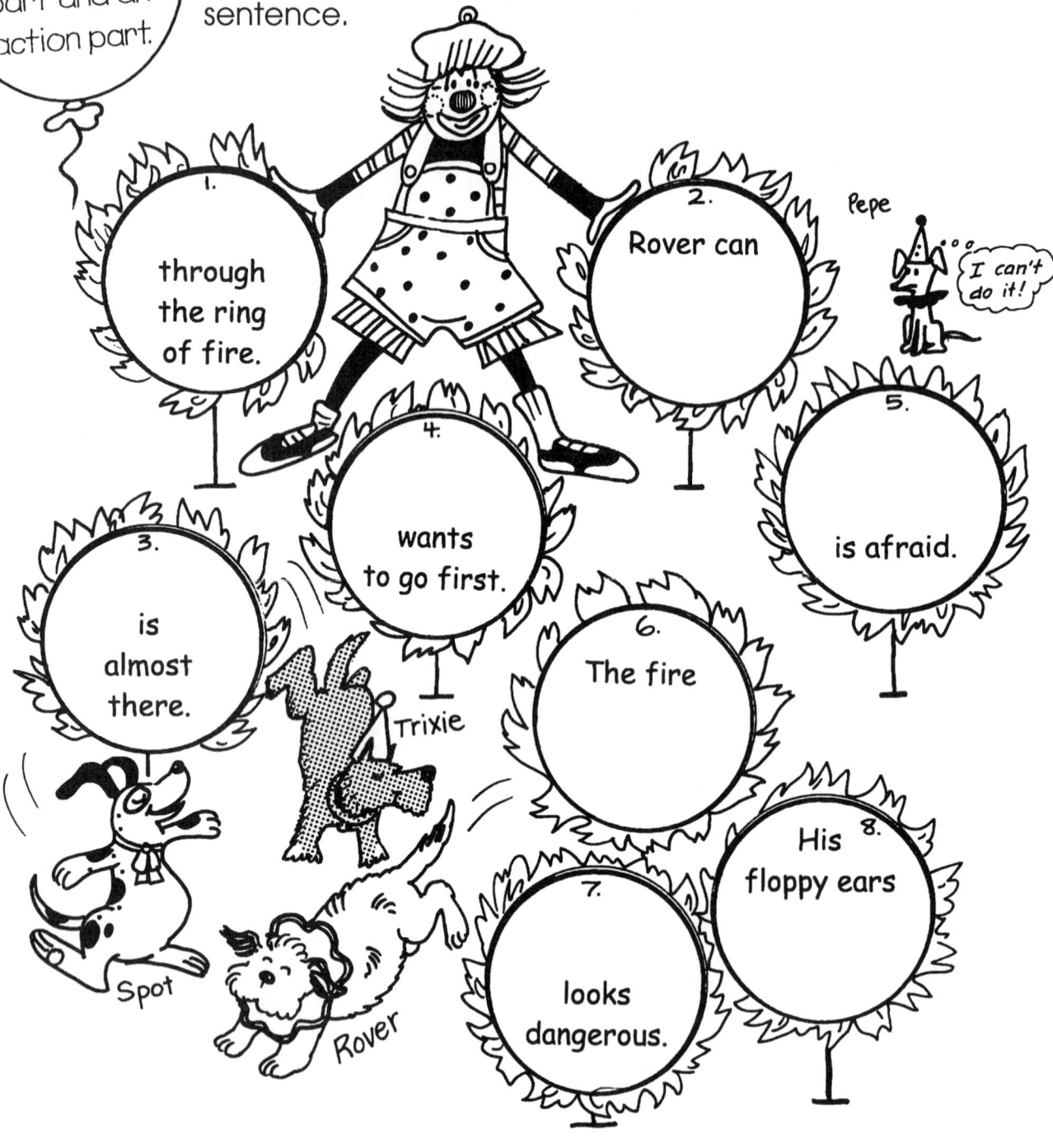

1. through the ring of fire.
2. Rover can
3. is almost there.
4. wants to go first.
5. is afraid.
6. The fire
7. looks dangerous.
8. His floppy ears

Pepe: I can't do it!

Name _____

Complete Sentences

Ring around Run-ons

The ring toss is a favorite game of the Clown-around Kids. Zeke and Zelda are always arguing about who is the best. Today they are trying to get rings around the bottles that have certain numbers. Help them out!

A run-on sentence runs two complete sentences together.

First, decide which sentences are run-ons. Fix them!
Then draw a ring around the bottles with the numbers of the run-on sentences.

1. Zeke threw the rings wildly, without aiming.
2. Zelda threw three rings around three bottles then she got a prize.
3. A radio was the prize she chose it was the best prize of all.
4. Even though Zeke was not careful, he won two games.
5. Step right up play the most exciting game throw rings around bottles
6. Did Zelda spend all her money did Zeke win anything?
7. Who won twenty free rides on the roller coaster?
8. Would Zeke be happy if he won the stuffed boa constrictor?
9. Only one ring went on the bottle the other nine flew out of the booth.
10. Who is the best at the ring toss anyway is it Zeke or Zelda?

How many rings did you draw? _____

Name _____

Copyright ©1998 by Incentive Publications, Inc., Nashville, TN.
Basic Skills/Language, Writing, & Usage 2-3

Run-on Sentences

23

Ribbons around Run-ons

The carnival has a show with acrobatic ribbon dancers. Rita and Rizzo are the best! It may look easy, but it is not! They leap over the ribbons while they do flips and amazing tricks. And the ribbons never get tangled!

*A **run-on sentence** runs two complete sentences together.*

Add a ribbon to one of the sticks each time you find a run-on sentence. Draw the ribbon from the stick around the run-on sentence. Then fix the sentence by putting in the right punctuation and capitals.

1. Rita and Rizzo can control twelve moving ribbons at once!
2. They leap over the ribbons they do somersaults under the ribbons.
3. These ribbon dancers are as talented as any other acrobats.
4. Can they twirl the ribbons from their toes can they close their eyes?
5. The audience was so surprised that their popcorn flew out of their hands.
6. Rita and Rizzo make ribbon hoops after that they jump through them.
7. The dancers surprised everyone they ate cotton candy while they danced.
8. Have you ever tried to do cartwheels while spinning ribbons with one hand?

Name _____

Inside the Lion's Mouth

*A **statement** is a telling sentence. It ends with a period.*

Would you have the nerve to do this?
Is Rollo being brave or foolish?

Read the story to find out what is going on!

As you read the sentences that tell the story, look for statements.

If a sentence is a statement, put a check on the line at the beginning of the sentence and a period at the end of it.

_____ 1. "Who is afraid of me"

_____ 2. This is the question Lester the lion asked the clowns

_____ 3. Everyone was silent

_____ 4. The clowns were so afraid, they couldn't even talk to the lion

_____ 5. They thought he might eat them if they said they were afraid

_____ 6. They thought he might eat them if they said they were **not** afraid

_____ 7. What happened then

_____ 8. Rollo offered his banana to the lion

_____ 9. Do lions like bananas

_____10. Let's hope so

_____11. Lester and Rollo became friends

_____12. Rollo showed the other clowns how much he trusted Lester by putting his head in the lion's mouth

_____13. Was this a good idea

_____14. What do you think happened next

Name _____

Copyright ©1998 by Incentive Publications, Inc., Nashville, TN.
Basic Skills/Language, Writing, & Usage 2-3

Statements

Unusual Talents

Ellie, the elephant, might have some unusual talents. It is possible she can do the things her friends say she can, but we can't be sure!

Change each statement about Ellie into a question to show that you wonder if she really does have these talents!

A question asks something. It ends with a ?

Ellie walks on the high wire.

Does Ellie walk on the high wire?

Can I believe my eyes?

Write each statement as a question.

1. That is Ellie on the high wire.
   _____

2. It is true that the elephant can fly.
   _____

3. Ellie can juggle pies.
   _____

4. Ellie knows how to ride a unicycle.
   _____

5. The elephant jumped through a ring of fire.
   _____

6. Ellie ate all the cotton candy.
   _____

Name _____

Watch out for Pirates!

Don't you love this ride! It's the best one at the carnival! Watch out for pirates, the shark, and the plank! Read all the things being said on the pirate ship. Color all the bubbles that contain exclamations.

An *exclamation* shows strong feeling. It ends with a !

- Save a bone for an old Sea Dog.
- Ahoy, maties!
- There's a ship on the horizon.
- Look out below!
- Shiver me timbers, I'm going to be sick!
- I am so scared of heights.
- Man overboard!!
- Wow! I found some pirate booty! Oh, boy!
- Arrrrggggh! Don't make me jump!!
- Just take one more step.
- Oh, no! I'm a goner!
- Help me, Mommy!
- Booty

CLOWN-AROUND PIRATE SHIP
OPEN 9 A.M. - 6 P.M.
Please do not feed the mechanical shark!

Name _____

Exclamations

A Bunch of Balloons

What kinds of sentences are in the balloons? Are they statements, questions, or exclamations? Do you know the difference?

Read each sentence. Add the correct punctuation.

Then color the balloons the right color:
Blue = statements   **Red** = questions   **Yellow** = exclamations

1. Is that clown crying
2. Look out for the dog
3. Don't pop my balloon
4. What a crazy costume
5. Where did you get those skates
6. Balloons come in five colors
7. Do these cost 50¢
8. The dog stands on his head
9. Oh, no My balloon popped
10. How many balloons are there

Name _____

Statements, Questions, & Exclamations

Seven Silly Seals

*Most sentences have a **subject** (noun part) and a **predicate** (verb part).*

Would seven silly seals throw tomatoes at parties? You decide!
The seal and the elephant have lists of sentence parts.
Every noun part (subject) needs a verb part (predicate).
Use a separate piece of paper to write ten sentences.
Use one sentence part from each list to write your sentences!

SUBJECTS

Seven silly seals
A nervous lion tamer
Fred the fire-eater
Four acrobats
Tina's pet snake
Four dancing bears
Elephants with wrinkles
The Clown-around Kids
The juggling brothers
Daring trapeze artists
Milton the Magnificent
Ten crazy monkeys

PREDICATES

swallows a sword!
ride prancing stallions.
stand on their heads.
eat French fried worms.
wear purple underwear.
blow bubbles in the bathtub.
gobbles red hot chili peppers.
tumble off the high wire.
looks in the lion's mouth.
tiptoe across a high wire.
leaps through a ring of fire.
throw tomatoes at parties.

Name _____

Sentence Parts

In the Center Ring

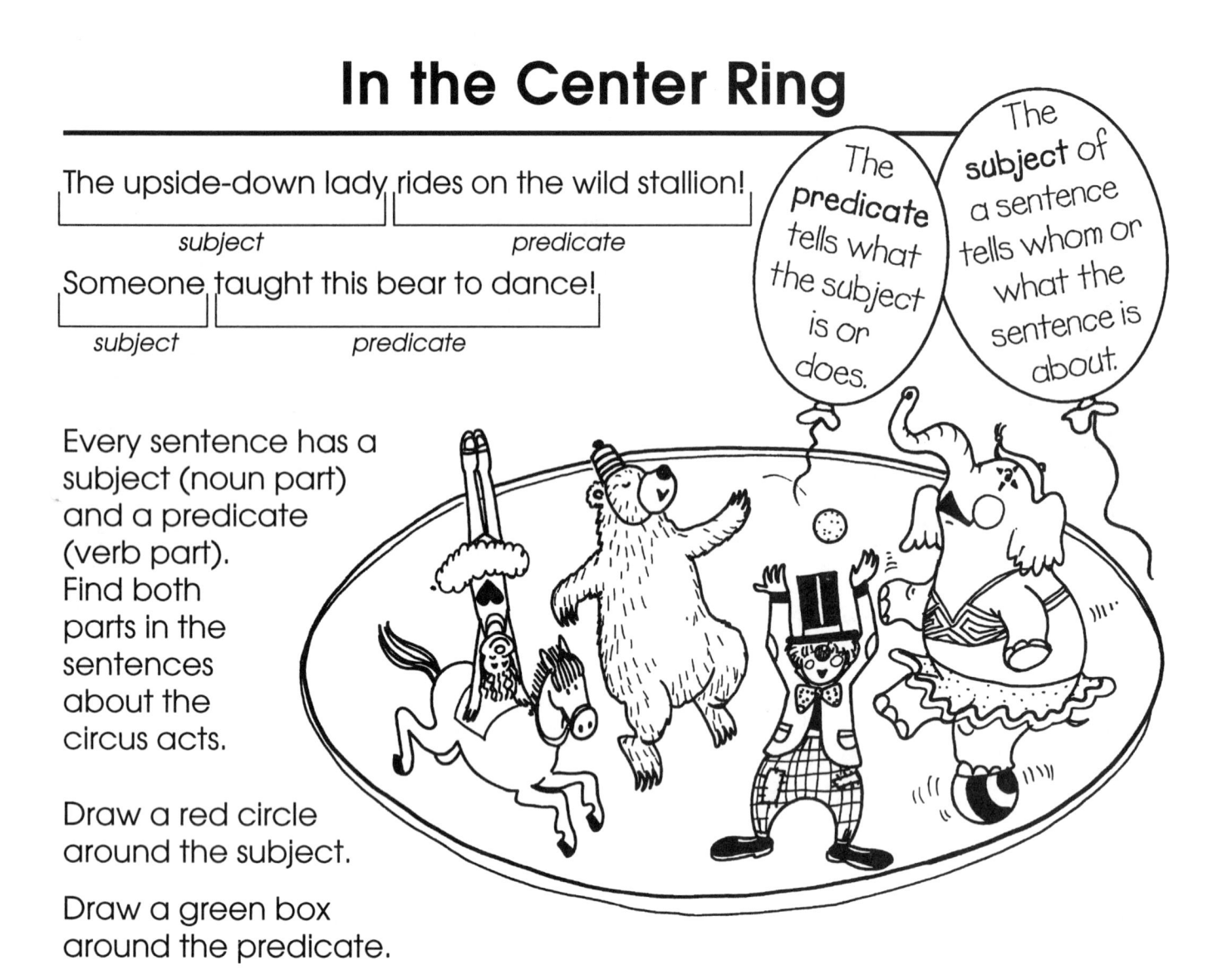

[The upside-down lady] [rides on the wild stallion!]
   subject   predicate

[Someone] [taught this bear to dance!]
 subject   predicate

The predicate tells what the subject is or does.

The subject of a sentence tells whom or what the sentence is about.

Every sentence has a subject (noun part) and a predicate (verb part). Find both parts in the sentences about the circus acts.

Draw a red circle around the subject.

Draw a green box around the predicate.

1. The balancing elephant is wearing a rather strange costume!
2. The clown juggles only one ball.
3. Only one bear was invited to be in the show today.
4. The other four elephants lost their costumes.
5. Ellie can stand on a ball with one foot for three minutes.
6. The galloping horse pays no attention to the lady on his back.
7. Clyde's pants need some more patches.
8. The audience wonders what is under the clown's hat.
9. A rather silly little hat sits on the bear's large head.
10. The center circus circle has four acts going on today.

Name _____

Sentence Parts

Juggling for Contractions

A contraction is two words squeezed together.

The juggling brothers, Gino and Georgie, have been practicing for years. They started with balls. Then they tried vegetables. Now they can juggle anything!

You can make contractions with the words on the things they are juggling.

Make a contraction to put into each blank in the sentences. Use the words from above to make the contractions. The same contraction may be used more than once.

1. Georgie _____ want to juggle toasters today.

2. He said _____ try again tomorrow.

3. "_____ start with five things each," said Gino.

4. The cake _____ fall to the ground once.

5. "_____ the best!" cried the audience.

6. Gino _____ using any vegetables in the show today.

7. They _____ do two shows today.

8. The show _____ last past four o'clock.

9. _____ they learn to juggle long ago?

10. "I _____ take my eyes off them!" said one visitor.

Name _____

Copyright ©1998 by Incentive Publications, Inc., Nashville, TN.
Basic Skills/Language, Writing, & Usage 2-3

Contractions

Ups & Downs

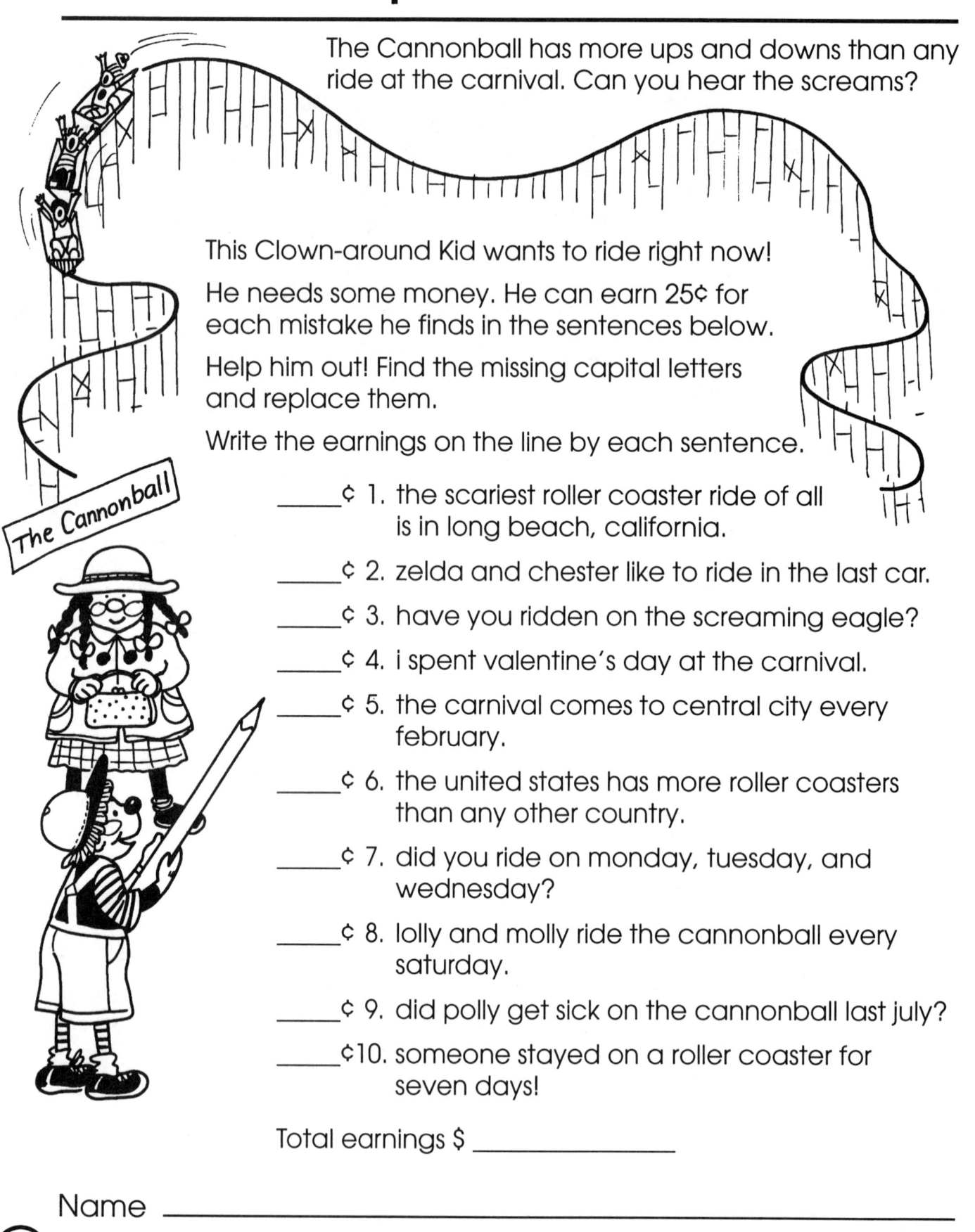

The Cannonball has more ups and downs than any ride at the carnival. Can you hear the screams?

This Clown-around Kid wants to ride right now!

He needs some money. He can earn 25¢ for each mistake he finds in the sentences below.

Help him out! Find the missing capital letters and replace them.

Write the earnings on the line by each sentence.

_____ ¢ 1. the scariest roller coaster ride of all is in long beach, california.

_____ ¢ 2. zelda and chester like to ride in the last car.

_____ ¢ 3. have you ridden on the screaming eagle?

_____ ¢ 4. i spent valentine's day at the carnival.

_____ ¢ 5. the carnival comes to central city every february.

_____ ¢ 6. the united states has more roller coasters than any other country.

_____ ¢ 7. did you ride on monday, tuesday, and wednesday?

_____ ¢ 8. lolly and molly ride the cannonball every saturday.

_____ ¢ 9. did polly get sick on the cannonball last july?

_____ ¢ 10. someone stayed on a roller coaster for seven days!

Total earnings $ _____

Name _____

32 Capitalization

Copyright ©1998 by Incentive Publications, Inc., Nashville, TN.
Basic Skills/Language, Writing, & Usage 2-3

Aim for the Ducks

How many ducks can the clowns hit at the arcade?
If they can hit all the ducks in two rows, they will win the prize of their choice!
Help them by following the directions below.

Find all the places where punctuation marks are missing and write them in.
Each time you use a mark, color a duck that has that punctuation mark.
Try to color at least two whole rows for the prize.

1. Ellie ate peanuts cotton candy and a funnel cake
2. Did you want to ride the Octopus
3. Oh no Now it's raining
4. Did the clown lose her nose
5. Hurry The show is starting
6. Please don't feed the monkeys
7. Mop Pop and Glop are clowns
8. The elephants stole the peanuts
9. Watch out for the tiger
10. Could you tame a lion
11. I can't wait to see the fire-eater
12. Well I think I have the tickets

Name _____

Quotes from the Circus Train

Quotation marks show the exact words someone says.

Speech bubbles from the illustration:
- "All aboard! Ride the Circus Town Express."
- "We like to go through the tunnels."
- "Can we go faster?"
- "Do we stop in Kalamazoo?"
- "This choo-choo is my favorite ride."

The people on the train all have some comments to make about the ride! Everything they are saying can be turned into sentences called quotations. Here's how! Tell who is speaking, and tell his or her exact words.

Put those exact words inside quotation marks. Put a comma after the quotation, unless it has a question mark or an exclamation point or is the end of the sentence.

Use the quotations above to finish these sentences.

1. _____"Can we go faster?"_____ asked Bubbles.

2. The engineer shouted, _____

3. _____ wondered Mrs. Clown.

4. Danno said, _____

5. _____ hollered the twins.

Name _____

Madame Mystery's Message

Look out below?
The trapeze clowns have a tricky act, they do twists. turns. and breath-taking flips, Is there anything they are afraid to do! They never fall? But watch out when they add the flying elephants to their act,

What a pickle!

Madam Mystery finds a strange and mysterious message in her mystery ball. It is interesting, but it is hard to read because it has so many mistakes. Write the message here. Correct the punctuation mistakes!

Name _____

Punctuation

Mistakes on the Merry-Go-Round

It is hard to resist a ride on a good merry-go-round!

This one is a favorite spot for the Clown-around Kids.

The merry-go-round could use some decoration!

Follow the directions to give it some color!

Circle the letters that should be capitalized, and add the correct punctuation. After you fix each sentence, color part of the ride.

Color

poles	1. bubbles rides the giraffe on fridays and saturdays
floor	2. do you like all that loud music
elephant	3. chester held onto a ring and rode standing up last june
giraffe	4. this ride has an elephant a giraffe and a unicorn
unicorn	5. reach for the ring
zebra	6. ulysses likes to ride on the unicorn on tuesdays
roof	7. is this carnival open on thanksgiving
clowns	8. does the carnival travel to chicago illinois

Name _____

36 Capitalization & Punctuation

Copyright ©1998 by Incentive Publications, Inc., Nashville, TN.
Basic Skills/Language, Writing, & Usage 2-3

A Letter to Ulysses

Ulysses, the unicycle rider, rode his unicycle to the mailbox and found a letter from his clown friend, Pretzel, who lives far away.

When you read the letter from Pretzel, you will see that he made a lot of mistakes.

Fix all the mistakes. Circle the letters that should be capitalized, and add punctuation in the correct places!

> dear ulysses
>
> i miss your smiling face i would have written sooner but i've been tied up the life of a famous contortionist can be knotty did you hear my news i've added a trick to my act you should see me do a double loop with a knee twist
>
> come and see me in florida
> your clown pal
> pretzel

I miss you, Pretzel.

Weird, Wacky Mirrors

Snuffles has wandered into the hall of wacky mirrors.
These mirrors make some things look strange or wrong!
In every mirror, some words are weird. They are not spelled right!
Use a red marker or crayon to circle all the words in the mirrors that are spelled correctly.

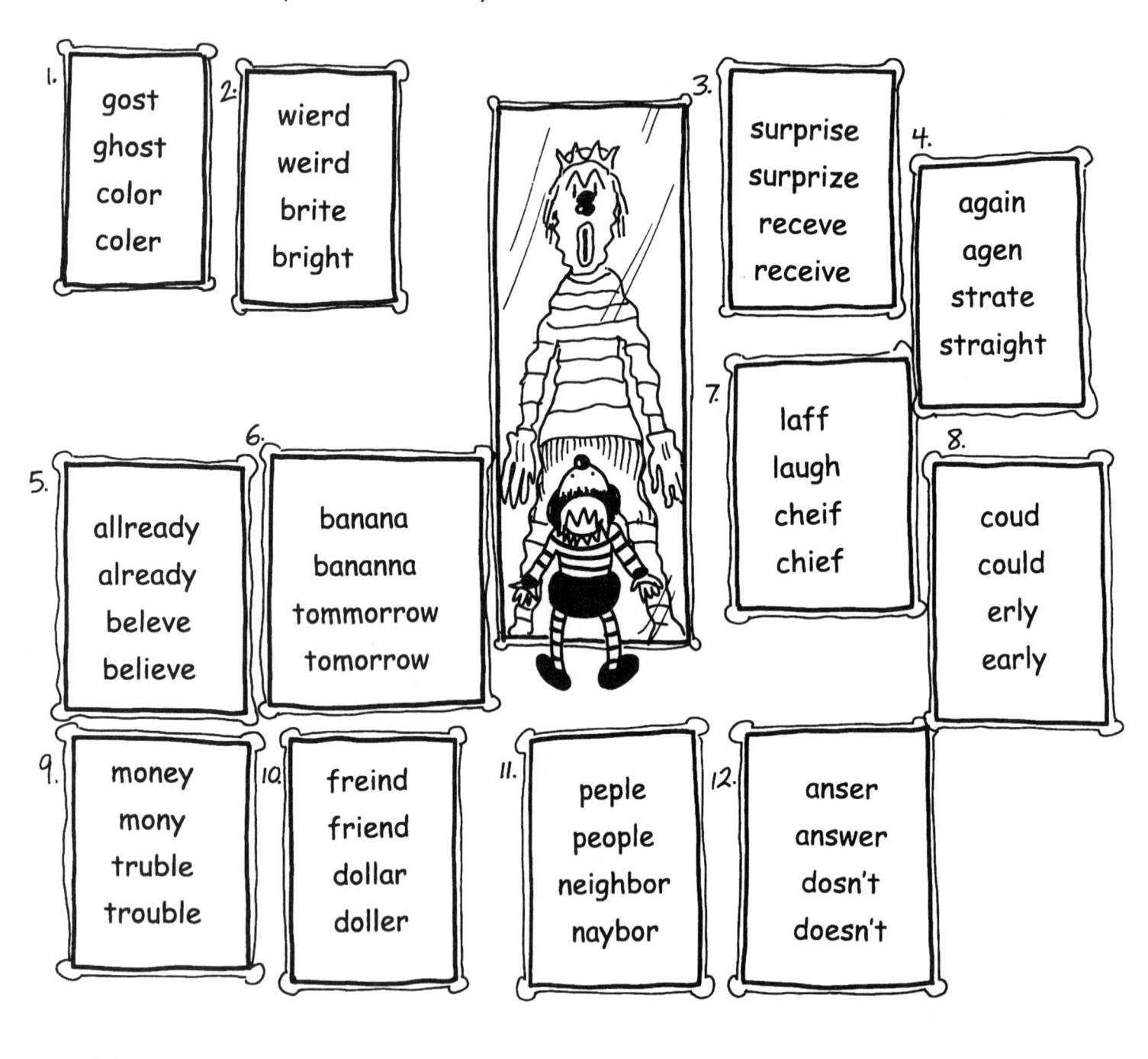

1. gost / ghost / color / coler
2. wierd / weird / brite / bright
3. surprise / surprize / receve / receive
4. again / agen / strate / straight
5. allready / already / beleve / believe
6. banana / bananna / tommorrow / tomorrow
7. laff / laugh / cheif / chief
8. coud / could / erly / early
9. money / mony / truble / trouble
10. freind / friend / dollar / doller
11. peple / people / neighbor / naybor
12. anser / answer / dosn't / doesn't

Name _____

38 Spelling

Copyright ©1998 by Incentive Publications, Inc., Nashville, TN.
Basic Skills/Language, Writing, & Usage 2-3

Dancing with a Bear

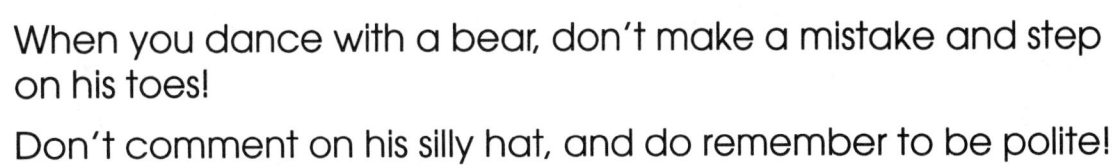

When you dance with a bear, don't make a mistake and step on his toes!

Don't comment on his silly hat, and do remember to be polite!

It's a good idea to try to avoid mistakes in spelling, too.

The sentences below each have at least one spelling mistake. Find the mistakes and write the words correctly on the line following the sentence.

1. How meny times have you danced with a grizzly bear?
   _____

2. Benjamin Bare likes to tell elefant jokes.

   _____

3. Evry other bear thinks Benjamin is funy. _____

4. Have you ever been steped on by a danceing bear?

   _____

5. Look! That bear is growling at those peple! _____

6. Have you wundered who taut these bears to dance?

   _____

7. Sumtimes the bears act allmost like humans. _____

8. Benjamin gets tried standing on his hinde legs. _____

9. Wuld you like a dancing bear for a pet? _____

Name _____

Spelling

Copyright ©1998 by Incentive Publications, Inc., Nashville, TN.
Basic Skills/Language, Writing, & Usage 2-3

Sniffing out Mistakes

It is Sniffy's job to track down misspelled words around the carnival grounds. He catches the words and pushes them into the trash can with his broom. Help him with his job by drawing a path for him to sweep. Draw a path that connects all the misspelled words.

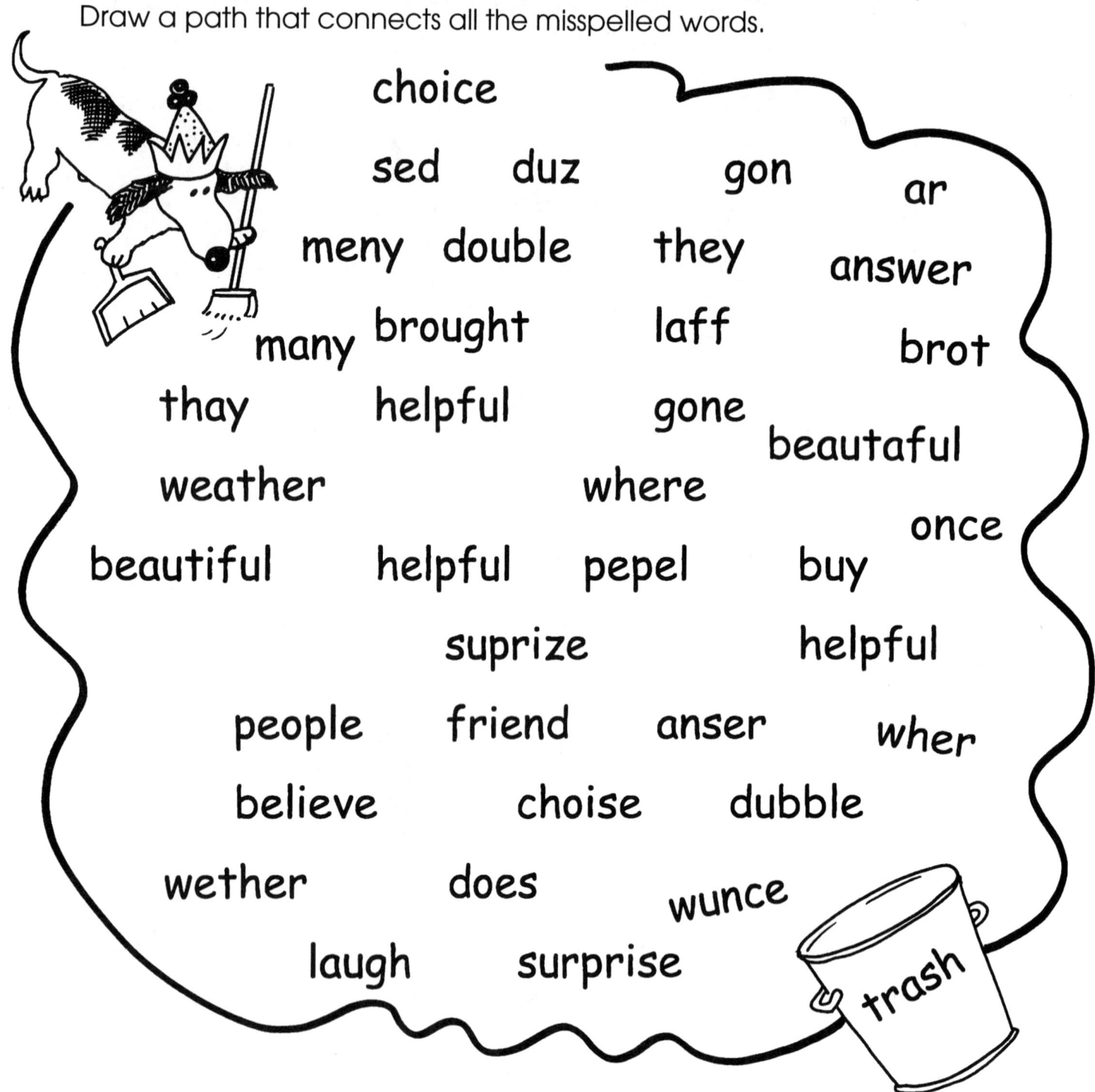

choice

sed   duz   gon   ar

meny   double   they   answer

many   brought   laff   brot

thay   helpful   gone
                              beautaful
weather   where
                                          once
beautiful   helpful   pepel   buy

suprize   helpful

people   friend   anser   wher

believe   choise   dubble

wether   does
                              wunce
laugh   surprise

trash

Name _____

Spelling

Wonderful Carnival Words

If you go looking, listening, and sniffing around the carnival, you will find some wonderful carnival words! These are words you could use to describe the sights, sounds, feelings, smells, and experiences of the carnival.

Look at each of the carnival pictures. Write some interesting or unusual words to describe each thing.

Yikes!
1. _____
2. _____
3. _____
4. _____
5. _____
6. _____

OOOPS!
1. _____ 4. _____
2. _____ 5. _____
3. _____ 6. _____

Mmmmm!
1. _____ 4. _____
2. _____ 5. _____
3. _____ 6. _____

Yawn!
1. _____ 4. _____
2. _____ 5. _____
3. _____ 6. _____

Name _____

Writing: Descriptive Words

Copyright ©1998 by Incentive Publications, Inc., Nashville, TN.
Basic Skills/Language, Writing, & Usage 2-3

Tempt Your Taste Buds

Cookie does some wonderful cooking!
Read her descriptions of three tasty treats.
Look for words that are ordinary or a little bit dull. Circle these.
Try to think of a better word to replace each one.
Make the new word more interesting, clever, fun, or unusual!

.... and for breakfast, scrumptious apple-butterscotch-cinnamon-flapjack-fritters!

Sundae on a Stick
It's a nice change!
The tasty vanilla ice cream is topped with good chocolate and dipped in little, chunky nuts.
It is cold and refreshing!

Sweet Cotton Candy
Come and get your pink fluffs of sugar candy on a paper cone.
It tastes so great that you will hurry back for more.

Hot Dogs
Hot dogs! Hot dogs!
Walk over to the hot dog stand and get your warm dogs right now.
Cover them with mustard, ketchup, or relish.
Try some fresh onions.

Name _____

Writing: Word Choice

Come One, Come All!

A poster is a great way to attract people to come to an event! Make your own poster to tell about one of the acts in the carnival or one of the carnival rides.

What _____

Time _____

Place _____

Date _____

Cost _____

Something great about the event!

_____

_____

_____

Come One, Come All!

BUMPER CAR RACE
at the BOARDWALK
6:00 pm
Every Wednesday
Prizes for the winners
Fun for Everyone
Near the Entrance

Name _____

Writing: Poster

Titles to Talk About

Great stories happen every day at the carnival.
These carnival stories have all lost their titles!
Write a new title for each story
on these two pages (44 and 45.)

_____

Step right up!
See the greatest show on Earth!
See jugglers, lions, and tigers!
See clowns and fire-eaters!
The tricks will amaze you!

_____

Zina Zardoom has squeezed her big feet into this tiny little car. How can she drive it without crashing into the lion cage? Good luck, Zina!

_____

Hungry Harry gets carried away with the circus treats. He can't stop eating popcorn, candy, and ice cream. His favorite treat of all is gooey, sticky, sugary cotton candy!

Name _____

Use with page 45.

Writing: Titles

Copyright ©1998 by Incentive Publications, Inc., Nashville, TN.
Basic Skills/Language, Writing, & Usage 2-3

_____

Ellie is all dressed up for the big show. She has on her favorite hat and her favorite ruffle. She wears her striped socks for good luck. What trick will she do tonight?

_____

Jugglers Gino and Georgie delight the crowd with their tricks. Their best trick is juggling vegetables. They take bites out of the vegetables. Then they throw them into the audience!

_____

This tricky monkey can hop, leap, stand on his head, and turn flips. He can throw his hat into the audience right onto someone's head! Then he scampers up on the person's shoulders to snatch back his hat!

Name _____

Use with page 44.

Writing: Titles

A Three-Ring Circus

A carnival is like a three-ring circus!
There is so much going on—all at once.
Collect some ideas about things that go on at the carnival.
Write down words and phrases—as many as you can think of.

FOODS I ATE...

FUNNY THINGS I SAW...

RIDES I TRIED...

Use some of your good ideas to write a story on the next page (page 47).

Name _____

Use with page 47.

Writing: Generating & Organizing Ideas

A Three-Ring Circus, cont.

Write your story on the lines below.

Tell what you did during a day at the carnival.

Include things you saw, did, and ate.

After you write your story, draw a picture to go along with it!

Draw a picture here.

_____
(Title)

Name _____

Use with page 46.

Writing: Generating & Organizing Ideas

A Chat with the Fire-Eater

Have you ever seen someone eat fire? Many carnivals have a person who does just that!

What would you ask a fire-eater if you could meet one?

Think of some questions you would ask him or her.

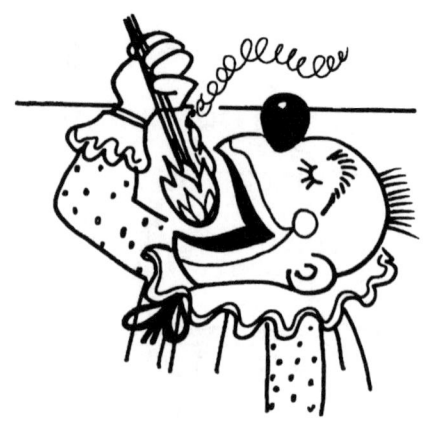

1. _____
2. _____
3. _____
4. _____
5. _____
6. _____
7. _____
8. _____

Choose one of your questions. Tell how you think the fire-eater might answer the question.

_____
_____
_____

Name _____

48

Writing: Interview Questions

Copyright ©1998 by Incentive Publications, Inc., Nashville, TN.
Basic Skills/Language, Writing, & Usage 2-3

Help for Handy

It's time for Handy to get ready to go to work. He wants to look dandy for the show. Help him decide how to get dressed. Write directions for Handy to tell him what to put on. Write your directions in order. Write complete sentences.

Curly Wig
Tattered Hat
Make-Up Kit
Red Nose
Gloves
Turtleneck Shirt
Favorite Vest
Knee Socks
Squirting Flower
Patched Pants
Umbrella
Rope Belt

1. _____
2. _____
3. _____
4. _____
5. _____
6. _____
7. _____
8. _____
9. _____
10. _____
11. _____
12. _____

Name _____

Copyright ©1998 by Incentive Publications, Inc., Nashville, TN.
Basic Skills/Language, Writing, & Usage 2-3

Writing: Directions

A Lion on the Loose!

There's a lion on the loose on the grounds of the carnival!
Look at the path the lion has taken to escape.
Write clear directions to tell the lion tamer how to follow the lion.
Use words such as *over, under, through, beside, across, behind, around, inside, in front of, north, south, east,* and *west.*

Name _____

Writing: Directions

Copyright ©1998 by Incentive Publications, Inc., Nashville, TN.
Basic Skills/Language, Writing, & Usage 2-3

Tina the Terrific

What is so terrific about Tina, the trapeze artist?
Read the beginning of her story.
Then finish it in an interesting way that will make others enjoy reading it!

When Tina was only two years old, she amazed her mom and dad. She amazed the neighborhood! She hung upside down in tall trees. She jumped down from high places. She even leaped off their _____ .

She couldn't wait _____

_____

_____

_____

_____

_____

_____

_____

_____

_____

Name _____

Writing: Finishing a Story

Fantastic Dreams

Snoozy is dreaming about a great trapeze trick he could do. What would your dream trick be?
Draw yourself doing the wildest trick you can imagine! Then write about it on the lines below.

Name _____

Writing: Imaginative Piece

A Letter from a Lion

Can you imagine a lion writing a letter? What would a lion say?
If Lester the Lion sent a letter to his friend, what do you think he would write?
Think about the things a lion does during a day. What might he hear, watch, wish, or think?
Write Lester's letter.

Dear Lillie,

Love,
Lester

Lester Lion
Clown-Around Circus

Lillie Lion
Happy Days Circus
Winter Camp, FL

Name _____

Writing: Letter

Copyright ©1998 by INCENTIVE PUBLICATIONS, Inc., Nashville, TN.
Basic Skills/Language, Writing, & Usage 2-3

Too Much of a Good Thing

The stories about the clowns at the carnival are full of good ideas, but every one of them has one idea too many!
Read each story on these two pages (pages 54 and 55).
Find the idea that is not needed in each story. Cross it out!

The Ticket Line

1. The Clown-around Kids have to wait in line to ride the Tilt-a-Whirl. It is their favorite ride, so they don't mind waiting.
After waiting for a long time, they reach the ticket window.
All the balloons fly into the air.
Zelda opens her purse and buys two tickets for everyone.
Then they enjoy a wild ride!

Ulysses Shows Off

2. Finally! Ulysses is ready to take the training wheels off his unicycle! He has invited all his friends to watch him perform. He is happy to show off. The monkey ate a bag of peanuts. Ulysses rides around the center ring without a spill. At last he is a true unicycle performer!

Name _____

Use with page 55.

Writing: Eliminating Irrelevant Ideas

Too Much of a Good Thing, cont.

Luscious Lion Treats

3. It's time for a lion treat! Cookie Clown is cooking up a special treat for her friend Lester Lion. She starts with chopped liver and adds onions and baked beans. She stirs in a dozen eggs and cooks it all for twenty minutes. Cookie washed her dishes. When the stew is done, she will call up Lester and invite him to lunch!

Prizes for Silly Clowns

4. Today is the Silly Clown Contest. The Clown-around Kids get into their silliest costumes and perform their silliest tricks. Zeke stands on his head. Zelda squirts people with her squirt-gun flower. Bubbles does some backwards somersaults. Henrietta walks on the tightrope with a glass of water on her head. Chester visited the elephants yesterday. All the Clown-arounds are very silly. Everybody wins a prize!

Name _____

Use with page 54.

Writing: Eliminating Irrelevant Ideas

Clowns up Close

Take a close-up look into the faces of the clowns!
Aren't they interesting characters?
A clown's face can tell you something about the personality of the clown.
Is the clown lazy, grumpy, silly, hungry, sad, happy, curious, troublesome, mischievous, or bothersome?
Try to match each clown with a name that shows the clown's personality.

Baby Cakes	Sweet-tooth Lou	Chatty Charo
Sorrowful Sam	Granny Annie	Angry Andy
Smart Art	Weary Willie	Silly Sid

Name _____

Use with page 57.

Writing: Character Descriptions

Clowns up Close, cont.

Choose one of the clowns on page 55. Write a description or story about the clown. Describe the clown's looks, tricks, activities, thoughts, or personality.

_____
_____
_____
_____
_____
_____
_____
_____
_____
_____

Write a story telling something your clown did.

Draw a clown face.

_____
_____
_____
_____
_____
_____
_____

Name _____

Use with page 56.

Writing: Character Descriptions

Language, Writing, & Usage Skills Test

1. Circle the words that can be nouns.
   - friendly
   - afternoon
   - trick
   - Friday
   - merry-go-round
   - Mrs. Clown
   - suddenly
   - gobbled
   - laughter

2. Circle the words that are proper nouns and should be capitalized.
   - easter
   - teacher
   - thursday
   - texas
   - mexico
   - boston
   - school

3. Circle the words in the magician's hat that can be verbs.

   swing   leaping   roar
   clown   laugh
   magic   tricks
   flying   tricked
        music
   grabbed   slowly

Draw a box around adjectives that describe nouns in these sentences.

4. Seven silly little clowns ate four bags of cotton candy.

5. Don't go near that fierce lion with the large teeth!

6. Which baby elephant has the broken toe?

7. Jennifer held her breath as she walked slowly across the thin, high wire.

Draw a box around the adverb that tells how, when, or where.

8. The tiger ate his lunch hungrily.

9. Four trapeze artists practice their tricks daily.

10. Circle the signs below that have complete sentences.

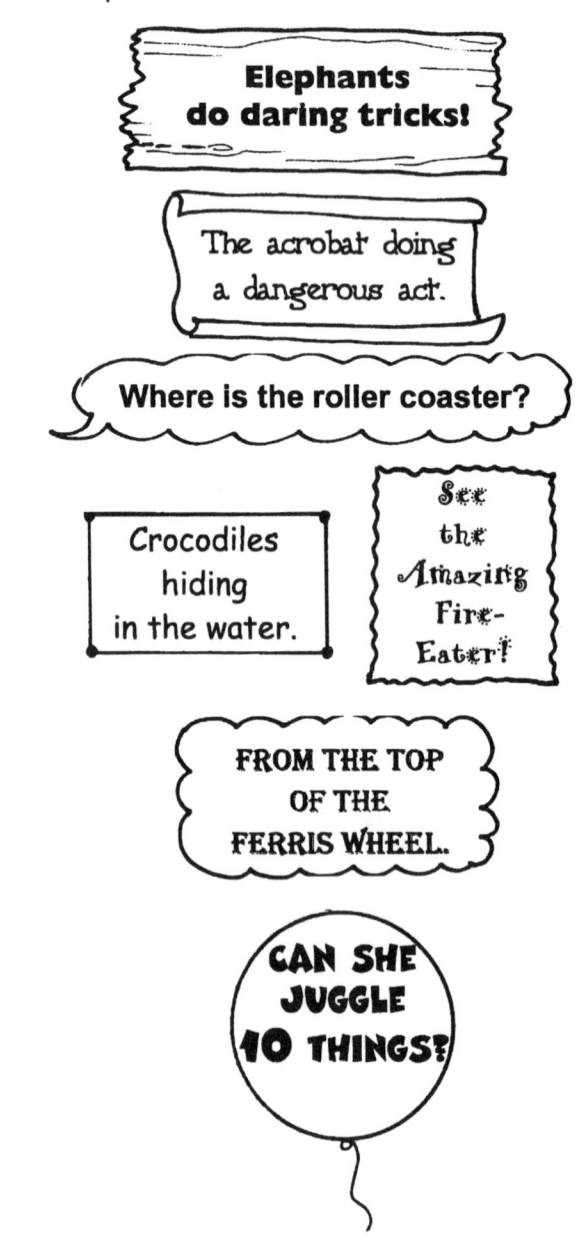

    - Elephants do daring tricks!
    - The acrobat doing a dangerous act.
    - Where is the roller coaster?
    - Crocodiles hiding in the water.
    - See the Amazing Fire-Eater!
    - FROM THE TOP OF THE FERRIS WHEEL.
    - CAN SHE JUGGLE 10 THINGS?

Name _____

11. Underline the sentence below that is a statement.

   Put a box around the sentence that is a question.

   Put a check mark in front of the sentence that is an exclamation.

   a. Can you ride a unicycle?

   b. Never put your hand in the tiger's cage!

   c. It is a good idea to be friendly to the gorillas.

Circle the numbers of the sentences that have correct punctuation.

12. Don't look down!

13. Which bear is good at dancing.

14. Did you try the giant hot dogs with grilled onions?

15. The juggler dropped a toaster on his head yesterday.

16. That is not a very good idea?

17. Circle the subject of the sentence.
    Two brave clowns jumped on the pirate ship this morning.

18. Circle the subject of the sentence.
    A nervous Gino put his head in the lion's mouth.

19. Circle the predicate of the sentence.
    The monkeys climbed all over their barrel.

20. Circle the predicate of the sentence.
    Chester, grab those balloons before they float away!

21. Circle the letters in Allie's envelope that should be capitalized.
    Add the missing punctuation.

   allie clown
   112 fun street
   central city iowa

   abby apricot
   2222 laughter lane
   cow's ear illinois 60001

22. Circle the letters in Allie's letter that should be capitalized.
    Add the missing punctuation.

   dear abby

   you won't believe the news the carnival came to our town last Thursday molly and i rode the roller coaster seven times we bought cotton candy four times guess what happened when I went to see the circus acts they invited me to be in the show they gave me the job of fire-eater it isn't all that hard—just a little hot

   love
   allie

Make a contraction from each of these pairs of words.

23. we will _____

24. they are _____

25. will not _____

Name _____

26. Circle the letters on the poster that should be capitalized. Add the missing punctuation.

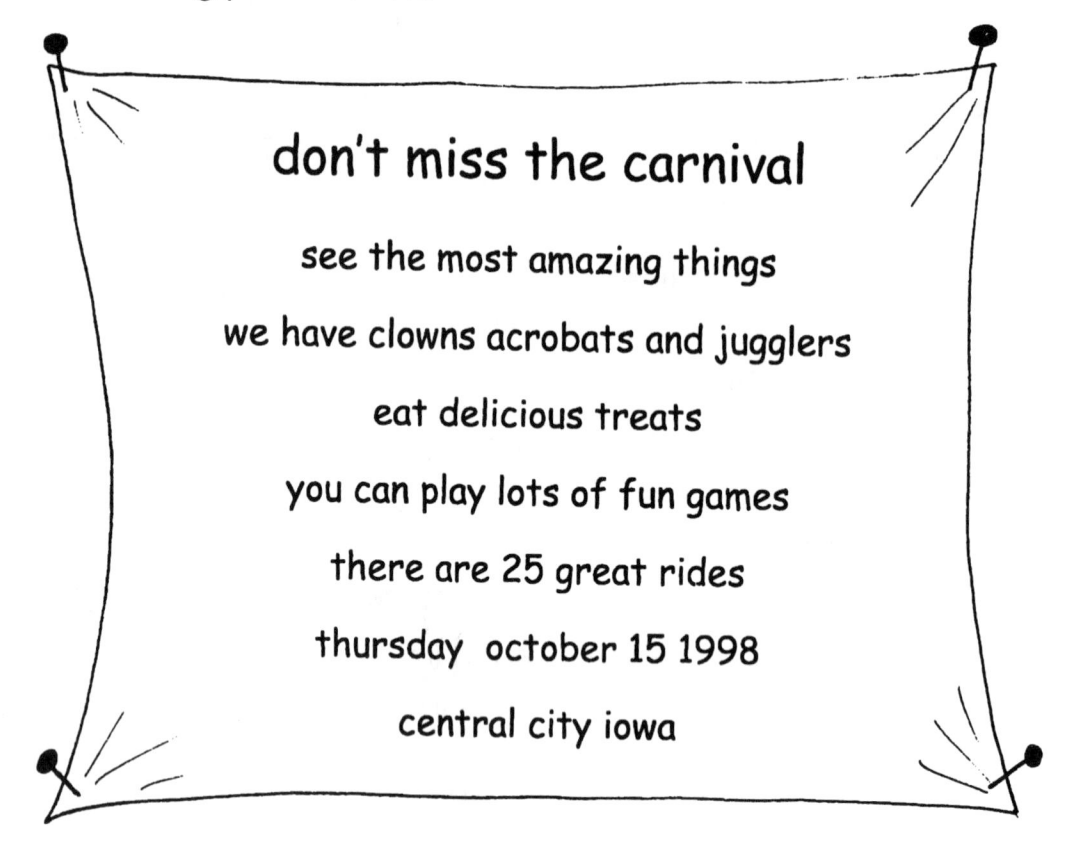

> don't miss the carnival
>
> see the most amazing things
>
> we have clowns acrobats and jugglers
>
> eat delicious treats
>
> you can play lots of fun games
>
> there are 25 great rides
>
> thursday october 15 1998
>
> central city iowa

27. Draw a line through the idea in this story that is not necessary.

   You won't believe what happened on the Pirate Ride today! Four visitors fell overboard! Three pirates had to walk the plank, and the mechanical shark sank. Everything was going wrong. Just then the circus show started. The sails fell down, too. Luckily, all the visitors thought these things were part of the ride. They laughed and laughed and said, "This is the best ride we've taken yet!"

28. Circle the title that would be best for the above story.
    a. Time to Walk the Plank
    b. The Mechanical Shark
    c. Trouble on the Pirate Ride
    d. Trouble at the Carnival

Name _____

29. Number the sentences in the correct order to build a story.

   _____ Then someone shouted, "Look out for that lion!"

   _____ Hundreds of people began to run and scream.

   _____ The lion tamer finally tracked Lester to the elephant pen.

   _____ Someone left the latch open on the lion cage door.

   _____ The clever lion escaped in no time.

   _____ At first no one noticed the lion wandering around.

   _____ He led Lester quietly back to the cage.

30. Choose one clown. Circle the one you chose. Imagine what this clown is like and what he or she might do, wear, or say!

   Give the clown a name. _____

   Write 6 words that describe what you imagine this clown to be like.

   1. _____   4. _____

   2. _____   5. _____

   3. _____   6. _____

   Write a sentence telling something the clown might do.

   _____

   _____

   _____

Name _____

Copyright ©1998 by INCENTIVE PUBLICATIONS, Inc., Nashville, TN.
Basic Skills/Language, Writing, & Usage 2-3

Language, Writing, & Usage Skills Test

Answer Key

Skills Test
1. Mrs. Clown, afternoon, trick, merry-go-round, Friday, laughter
2. Easter, Mexico, Boston, Thursday, Texas
3. swing, leaping, tricks, tricked, roar, laugh, grabbed, flying, clown
4. Seven, silly, little, four, cotton
5. fierce, large
6. baby, broken
7. thin, high
8. hungrily
9. daily
10. Elephants do daring tricks! See the Amazing Fire-Eater! Where is the roller coaster? Can she juggle 10 things?
11. a. box around it
    b. √ in front
    c. line under it
12. Circled
13. Not circled
14. Circled
15. Circled
16. Not circled
17. Two brave clowns
18. A nervous Gino
19. climbed all over their barrel
20. grab those balloons before they float away
21. Allie Clown
    112 Fun Street
    Central City, Iowa
    Abby Apricot
    2222 Laughter Lane
    Cow's Ear, Illinois
    60001
22. Dear Abby,
    You won't believe the news! The carnival came to our town last Thursday. Molly and I rode the roller coaster seven times. We bought cotton candy four times. Guess what happened when I went to see the circus acts? They invited me to be in the show! They gave me the job of fire-eater. It isn't all that hard—just a little hot!
    Love, Allie
23. we'll
24. they're
25. won't
26. Don't miss the carnival! See the most amazing things! We have clowns, acrobats, and jugglers. Eat delicious treats. (or !) You can play lots of fun games. There are 25 great rides. (or !) Thursday, October 15, 1998 Central City, Iowa
27. Just then the circus show started.
28. c
29. 4, 5, 6, 1, 2, 3, 7
30. See that student has completed all sections of the question.

Skills Exercises

pages 10–11
page 10—See that student has chosen nouns to name things pictured.
page 11—See that student has chosen verbs represented in the picture.

page 12
1. friend
2. umbrella
3. zebra
4. zoo
5. yaks
6. kitchen
7. iguana
8. tongue
9. teeth
10. eggs
11. nose
The surprise is a fuzzy kitten!

page 13
Mrs. Clown, Bellview School, Monday, October, Valentine's Day, Dallas, Texas, Rizzo, Main Street, Brooklyn Bridge, Milton, Colorado River, Thanksgiving, Friday, Leo, July

page 14
mice
bunnies
bears
knives
cameras
butterflies
puppies
turtles
fish (or fishes)
glasses
radios
monkeys
ducks
pennants
hippos

page 15
1–8. Add 's to all blanks.

pages 16–17
Down
1. teased
2. scratch
3. tickles
9. tumbled
10. roll
13. toss

Across
4. reach
5. flip
6. shake
7. skip
8. chatter
11. sobs
12. jump
14. flop
15. gobble

page 18
1. helped; skipped
2. talked; tripped
3. leaped; begged
4. trimmed; yelled
5. popped; trotted
6. crawled; jumped
yellow: cup 1, 2, 3, 6; saucer 4, 6
green: cup 4, 5; saucer 1, 2, 3, 5

page 19
1. lucky, purple, big—30 points
2. six, good—20 points
3. new, striped, important—30 points
4. first, nice, smooth, steady—40 points
5. Four, noisy, teenage—30 points

6. second, highest—20 points
7. big, pink, cotton—30 points
8. long, winning—20 points

Zelda's score was 220 points.

page 20
1. larger
2. biggest
3. taller, shorter
4. largest
5. longer
6. shorter
7. widest
8. littlest
9. redder
10. silliest

page 21
1. slowly
2. soon
3. down
4. Carefully
5. ahead
6. tightly
7. never
8. frequently
9. deeply
10. Soon
11. Suddenly
12. rapidly
13. safely
14. Tomorrow

page 22
Answers will vary. See that student has written complete sentences.

page 23
Rings around 2, 3, 5, 6, 9, 10; Total 6
See that student has correctly fixed the run-ons.

page 24
Ribbons around 2, 4, 6, 7
See that student has correctly fixed the run-ons.

page 25
Statements are 2, 3, 4, 5, 6, 8, 10, 11, 12.

page 26
Questions may vary somewhat.
1. Is that Ellie on the high wire?
2. Is it true that the elephant can fly?
3. Can Ellie juggle pies?
4. Does Ellie know how to ride a unicycle?
5. Did the elephant jump through a ring of fire?
6. Did Ellie eat all the cotton candy?

page 27
All bubbles are exclamations except:
Save a bone for an old sea dog.
Just take one more step.
There's a ship on the horizon.
I am so scared of heights.

page 28
Blue—statements should have periods at the ends: 6, 8
Red—questions should have question marks at the ends: 1, 5, 7, 10
Yellow—exclamations should have exclamation points: 2, 3, 4, 9

page 29
Answers will vary. See that students have formed 10 complete sentences.

page 30
1. S—The balancing elephant P—is wearing a rather strange costume!
2. S—The clown P—juggles only one ball.
3. S—Only one bear P—was invited to be in the show today.
4. S—The other four elephants P—lost their costumes.
5. S—Ellie P—can stand on a ball with one foot for three minutes.
6. S—The galloping horse P—pays no attention to the lady on his back.
7. S—Clyde's pants P—need some more patches.
8. S—The audience P—wonders what is under the clown's hat.
9. S—A rather silly little hat P—sits on the bear's large head.
10. S—The center circus circle P—has four acts going on today.

page 31
Answers will vary. See that student has written a contraction in each space and that the sentence makes sense.

page 32
1. The, Long, Beach, California—100¢
2. Zelda, Chester—50¢
3. Have, Screaming, Eagle—75¢
4. I, Valentine's, Day—75¢
5. The, Central, City, February—100¢
6. The, United, States—75¢
7. Did, Monday, Tuesday, Wednesday—100¢
8. Lolly, Molly, Cannonball, Saturday—100¢
9. Did, Polly, Cannonball, July—100¢
10. Someone—25¢

Total $8.00

page 33
Students should color in most of the ducks.
1. Ellie ate peanuts, cotton candy, and a funnel cake.
2. Did you want to ride the Octopus?
3. Oh, no! Now it's raining!
4. Did the clown lose her nose?
5. Hurry! The show is starting! (or .)
6. Please don't feed the monkeys! (or .)
7. Mop, Pop, and Glop are clowns.
8. The elephants stole the peanuts. (or !)
9. Watch out for the tiger!

10. Could you tame a lion?
11. I can't wait to see the fire-eater! (or .)
12. Well, I think I have the tickets.

page 34
Answers may vary somewhat.
1. "Can we go faster?" asked Bubbles.
2. The engineer shouted, "All aboard! Ride the Circus Town Express."
3. "Do we stop in Kalamazoo?" wondered Mrs. Clown.
4. Danno said, "This choo-choo is my favorite ride."
5. "We like to go through tunnels," hollered the twins.

page 35
Look out below! The trapeze clowns have a tricky act. They do twists, turns, and breath-taking flips. Is there anything they are afraid to do? They never fall, but watch out when they add the flying elephants to their act!

page 36
1. Bubbles rides the giraffe on Fridays and Saturdays.
2. Do you like all that loud music?
3. Chester held onto a ring and rode standing up last June.
4. This ride has an elephant, a giraffe, and a unicorn.
5. Reach for the ring!
6. Ulysses likes to ride on the unicorn on Tuesdays.
7. Is this carnival open on Thanksgiving?
8. Does the carnival travel to Chicago, Illinois?

page 37
Punctuation may vary. Some sentences may be seen as exclamations or statements.
Dear Ulysses,
I miss your smiling face. I would have written sooner, but I've been tied up. The life of a famous contortionist can be knotty! Did you hear my news? I've added a trick to my act. You should see me do a double loop with a knee twist! Come and see me in Florida.
Your clown pal,
Pretzel

page 38
Correct words are:
1. ghost, color
2. weird, bright
3. surprise, receive
4. again, straight
5. already, believe
6. banana, tomorrow
7. laugh, chief
8. could, early
9. money, trouble
10. friend, dollar
11. people, neighbor
12. answer, doesn't

page 39
1. many
2. Bear, elephant
3. Every, funny
4. stepped, dancing
5. people
6. wondered, taught
7. Sometimes, almost
8. tired, hind
9. Would

page 40
Exact paths may vary. Misspelled words are:
meny
sed
duz
gon
ar
brot
laff
thay
pepel
beautaful
wher
anser
suprize
wether
choise
dubble
wunce

page 41
See that student has written words in every category.

page 42
See that student has chosen dull words and replaced them with interesting words.

page 43
See that student has complete poster including all the information asked.

pages 44–45
See that student has written an appropriate title for each passage.

pages 46–47
See that student has completed both pages, collecting ideas and using some for the writing on page 47.

page 48
See that student has completed all sections with reasonable questions.

page 49
See that student has given logical, clear, sequential directions.

page 50
See that student has given logical, clear, sequential directions that match the map.

page 51
See that student has finished story in a way that is complete and makes sense.

page 52
See that student has described and illustrated a trick.

page 53
See that student has written an adequate letter with some detail.

pages 54–55
Irrelevant sentences are:
1. All the balloons fly into the air.
2. The monkey ate a bag of peanuts.
3. Cookie washed her dishes.
4. Chester visited the elephants yesterday.

pages 56–57
See that student has adequately completed all tasks.